Poetic Melodies

Creative Talents Unleashed

GENERAL INFORMATION

Poetic Melodies

By

Creative Talents Unleashed

1st Edition: 2016

This Publishing is protected under Copyright Law as a "Collection". All rights for all submissions are retained by the Individual Author and or Artist. No part of this publishing may be Reproduced, Transferred in any manner without the prior **WRITTEN CONSENT** of the "Material Owner" or it's Representative Creative Talents Unleashed.

Creative Talents Unleashed

www.ctupublishinggroup.com

Publisher Information
1st Edition: Creative Talents Unleashed
CreativeTalentsUnleashed@aol.com

This Collection is protected under U.S. and International Copyright laws

Copyright © 2016: Creative Talents Unleashed

ISBN-13: 978-0692739754 (Creative Talents Unleashed)
ISBN-10: 0692739750

$13.95

Credits

Book Cover

Donna J. Sanders

Editor

Authors Responsible For Own Work

Preface

Christopher Allen Breidinger

Preface

There is a human language that encompasses the globe, regardless of race, color, creed or country. Much the same way as laughter or tears, or any of our human emotions. When we see someone laugh, there is a universal language that is communicated by all of us. We know they are happy. Just as when we see someone crying, it is generally accepted to mean they are, most likely, sad. However, the language I am referring to goes beyond the sight of emotions, and runs deeper than the tear streaked lines of a sad face. I am speaking of a language that can penetrate to the deepest depths of the human psyche, it can be felt in the beating of our hearts and it can leave us soaring among our dreams.

This universal language is music.

Upon these waves of sound we can find our spirits lifted to the heavens, we can feel the beats and the rhythms in our beings and we are moved by the vibrations. We may become lost in a memory or a moment of time may be singled out by the distinct patterns and oscillations of a melody. We may gather by the thousands to listen to this music together or we may be alone in our rooms, or be dancing with our friends or cuddling with our love, but the universal language of music expands human communication beyond the normal realm. It propels us into the wavelengths of our souls, and it is there that we become in tune, we find our harmonies, and we recognize that there is a true power in music.

The poetry included in this book seeks to capture that essence and tap into that power. These are the lines of communication opened and inspired by the universal language called music.

Christopher Allen Breidinger, *Author*

Table of Contents

Preface   v

Sound Tracks

The Beat of My Heart *Shirley Ann Cooper*	3
Love Song *Stephanie Francis*	4
Music is Life *Vincent Van Ross*	5
When A Song Opened My Eyes *D.B. Hall*	7
Out to Lunch *Victor Clevenger*	10
That Song *Jennifer Criss*	11
Wilderness *Jimmy Boom Semtex*	12

Table of Contents

Remember When   13
Renee Furlow

Journey   14
Steve Lay

Musical Influence   15
Leon Pryce

Lullaby   17
Donna J. Sanders

Rhymes Rebirth   19
Christena AV Williams

Soundtrack   21
Lynn White

Harmonies

Sunshine Song   25
Scott Thomas Outlar

When She Sings   26
D.B. Hall

The Poet's Harmony   28
Christopher Allen Breidinger

Table of Contents

Switchblade Songbird   29
Billy Charles Root

Molded in Song   31
William L. Wright, Jr.

Music in the House   32
Sunayna Pal

Melodious in B Major   34
Ken Allan Dronsfield

I Dream in Symphonies   35
Don Beukes

Unsung Sonnet   37
Heath Brougher

Secluded Notes   38
Billy Charles Root

Rhythm   40
C. Steven Blue

Every Heart has a Poetic Melody   42
Mark Andrew Heathcote

Starting Over   43
Tammy T. Stone

Music   45
Sue Lobo

Table of Contents

Among the Unfulfilled   46
William L. Wright, Jr.

Harmony   48
Lynn White

Instruments

Violin   51
Donna J. Sanders

Ode to the Talking Drum   52
Olawale Famodun

Melodic Memories   53
Elizabeth Daniel

Life Is A Piano   54
Elizabeth Esguerra Castillo

Finger Jams   55
Raja Williams

Enchanted Flute   56
Baidha Fercoq

Fingering Strings   57
Victor Clevenger

Table of Contents

Piano   58
Maggie Mae Carter

My Spanish Guitar   59
Shirley Ann Cooper

First Love   61
Teresa Roberts

Sounds of the Drums   62
Leon Pryce

Spectral Violin   64
Baidha Fercoq

Trumpet   65
Maggie Mae Carter

African Drums   66
Sue Lobo

Instrument   67
Maggie Mae Carter

Soul Sounds

Humanity Sings   71
Tamsen Grace

Table of Contents

Music at Dusk   73
D.B. Hall

Nature's Opus   75
Don Beukes

The Voice of Heart   77
Rashmi Jain

Celestial Crescendo   78
Scott Thomas Outlar

Background Noise   79
L. J. Diaz

Music of Life   80
Rashmi Jain

Dancing to a Heart Song   81
Ken Allan Dronsfield

Musical String Theory   82
Valormore De Plume

Music of the Monsoons   83
Debasish Mishra

Spirituality   84
Vincent Van Ross

The Calling   86
Teresa Roberts

Table of Contents

Soul Strumming   87
Adam Levon Brown

Artist Tributes

Song for Karen   91
Don Beukes

One World In Harmony   93
C. Steven Blue

Purple   94
Maggie Mae Carter

My Quest   95
Veronica "Vee" Thornton

Eazy-E   96
Isiah Williams

Ode to Jimi Hendrix   97
Christopher Allen Breidinger

The Man   98
Veronica "Vee" Thornton

Love Letter to the Beatles   99
Kelly Klein

Table of Contents

Comfortably Numb   101
Shirlry Ann Cooper

Cry Goodbye   102
Christa Frazee

Ode to Mridangam Master   103
Caroline Nazareno-Gabis (Ceri Naz)

Mars Piper: A Poem For SYD Barrett   104
Julius Howard

Under the Influence of Bob Marley   106
Christena AV Williams

Gardenia   107
Christa Frazee

Tracy Chapman   108
Christena AV Williams

I'm in Love with a Country Man: Homage to   110
John Denver - *Sue Lobo*

Janis   111
Lynn White

The Starving Artist Fund   114
Our Links   116

Poetic Melodies

Creative Talents Unleashed

Sound Tracks

Poetic Melodies

The Beat of My Heart

While I lay in bed comfortably in a dream,
The world outside isn't what it seems.
The butterflies flutter like music notes,
The sound of acoustic begins to flow.
How my heart starts to race with every strum,
Then it becomes stronger than drums.
Rain falls hard like the sound of the harp,
Thunder rolls like an electric guitar.
I run after you my passionate pursuit,
I need to feel all of you.
The desires of my heart cry out loud,
Embracing me like a musical cloud.
I feel turned out like an old radio on a shelf,
I can't get a hold of myself.
I need you so much,
Where is your touch.
Like a piano needs its keys,
I need you with me.
Through the wildflowers I hear you,
Your voice is on cue.
Like streams of living water through me,
Are the sounds of a hundred tambourines.
You are the piece to my every instrument,
My ears are filled with pure excitement.
I will chase you forever,
We will one day sing together.
You are my life's music sheet,
The notes that make my heart beat.

Shirley Ann Cooper

Love Song

I dream of hearing the love song you sang to me when we first met. Almost like a symphony of colors that keep my heart connected to you. Those words unspoken leave me speechless and helpless to the strings you play on my heart. You give to me that music my soul craves. I want to live and breathe in your love song every day of my life.

Stephanie Francis

Music is Life

Please switch on
The tape recorder
And press
The 'Play' button—
Let the music begin…

Do not touch
The pause,
Fast forward,
Stop,
Eject,
Or, the Rewind buttons

Let the music flow
The way it is—
At its own pace

I do not
Wish to rush
Into my future
By pressing
The 'Fast Forward' button

Nor,
Do I want to retrace
My steps
Into my hoary past
With the 'Rewind' button

I want
To live
In the present moment
I want to enjoy it

Poetic Melodies

So, just press the 'Play' button
And, leave it there

Let the music play
As it always does
I want to
Take life as it comes
Let me take my life
In my stride

I do not
Want to pause,
Stop,
Eject,
Fast forward,
Or, rewind my life

I just want
To unwind
And enjoy
The music
For what
It is worth
Because,
Music
Is life

Vincent Van Ross

When A Song Opened My Eyes

Every moment spent waiting
at this dirty Bolivian stop
waiting for a brightly colored bus
to come rolling up
through the searing heat
is spent listening to boring tunes
playing on the tienda's radio.

A brightly colored bus pulls up
and the music changes
to something that really caught my imagination
I'm not sure who it is
I hear "Man In The Mirror"
and I'm hooked
as I climb on board
and head down to the post office.

A lot of Spanish people
were nodding to the beat of this English song
I wonder if they understand the words
and I wonder if English people
understand the message;
myself, I was finally seeing
the beggars on the street
how many times have I walked by
averting my proud eye.

I found out who the singer was,
Michael Jackson
and his beautiful song
have stuck with me to this day.

From all his hits like Bad

Poetic Melodies

Billy Jean
Smooth Criminal
Dirty Diana
Black or White
to The Way You Make Me Feel
there was always something
in his music
that connected with me.

But till the end of my days
that first song
heard in a packed bus
on a cobblestone street in South America
will always be the one
that really grabs my ear
it will always be my favorite one
where the King of Pop
asks the man in the mirror
to change his ways.

Hard Times and Dangerous Curves

Life gets hard
unbelievably hard at times
and yes
it gets to me
oh yes it does indeed.

Makes me want to drive
listen to Metallica
cranking some angry hard guitar riffs
push the gas pedal through

Poetic Melodies

the floor
and be the angry hog
filled with road rage.

But once I get home
with my laptop screen flipped up
and my earbuds in
I've started listening
to more and more blues
still love those guitar riffs
but they seem
so much cooler
coming from a guitar named Lucille

B.B. King made her talk so sweet
Clapton and SRV,
dudes with nicknames like Mississippi
T-Bone
Howling Wolf
and Muddy Waters
how could it not be cool?

I let these wise old souls
tell me their stories
of dangerous work
of dangerous curves
and love that lost
before it's been found
yeah I let them sing me their sorrows
I let them sing me the blues
and it takes me to a better place

D.B. Hall

Out to Lunch

She wondered why I never smiled like the piano man smiled, sitting in the corner fingering ivory and I wondered

why she never danced like the other fat women danced, on wooden floors in flat shoes; we both had our own reasons

not to, I suppose, but as Love Dream by Liszt began to play, I took the opportunity to explain to her that, "Before

alcoholism, my toughest addiction was my love for the manic inside of a depressive woman." "Is that why you

never smile?" she replied. "No," I told her, "I never smile because it makes me look tough, like a Chicago steel

worker in the winter of 1943." "But you never really look tough," she said, "You just look angry." The piano man

finished Love Dream and everyone applauded softly; the waitress served our tomato bread soup.

Victor Clevenger

That Song

It's that song-
the one she tried so hard to avoid
and made her think of him.
It assaulted her as she carefully fingered
the fabric of a skirt on the clearance rack.
It's that song they danced to as the rain poured down on them
after everyone else had sought shelter, soaking them to the bone.
It's that song- the one he'd sing in her ear softly,
trying to wake her on Sunday morning.
It's that song-
Memories she'd blocked out began to
seep in around the edges
and so began the waterfall of tears.
For so long the dam had held them back, but the floodgates had opened.
It's that song.
She left the shop leaving her cart and the floral skirt behind
In the middle of the aisle.

Jennifer Criss

Wilderness

We finally finished our album.
I'm so happy.
It will be on sale in 200 record shops in Norway.
I hope our music speaks to people.
I want them to experience that feeling when they listen to it.
I want to change things.
I'm not sure if my band members feel it or would agree with that?
I can touch that feeling,
like something's being born.
I know it's possible and with luck will happen.
My record, my singing, my words changing things
and setting Norway on her new path.
In a hundred years when I'm just dust,
people will remember me and my record.
I started the revolution from within.
The wilderness understands.

Jimmy Boom Semtex

Remember When

It began fast as I saw right though you.
The hint of music resonated through
everything we did.
There was plenty I knew about you,
but just as much that I didn't.
Sharing melodies was the only way inside
and finding the right ones were never hard.
Because when it came to you,
it was always the right song.
The lyrics took me to a place of becoming
and your eyes took me to a
very different way of doing the same.
This became my heaven, in and out,
and no one needed to understand.
The cool waters you brought me to
sent me to the place where it matters.
So much time has passed,
but those songs,
that music,
those lyrics –
they linger on.
And as much as we try to forget,
as much as we try to remember –
we are always transported
when the music permeates the space
and the right words come forth
at the right time
and I must ask –
may we sing a duet?

Renee Furlow

Journey

Come home from work after a long day,
Working so hard for a low pay,
Lie on my bed headphones turned on,
I drift away into a world of song,
Suddenly I start to feel light,
Close my eyes my dreams take flight,
Feel the beat of the drum in your heart,
As the music takes control,
Nothing hurts your soul,
Let nothing take control,
Nothing hurts as you flirt with the notes that someone wrote,
As you feel like they are being sung to you,
Feel yourself lifted of the ground,
Sail down the river of sound.

Steve Lay

Musical Influence

I`m under the influence of music
Music is my drug
I`m so addicted to it

I hear the words
And all I do is keep writing
I never cease
Because there is no ease
I get so inspired
With words like these
So keep it playing
Keep on singing
While I write my heart out
On these pages
Because i`m under the influence
Of music

I had no vision
But now I see clear
My mind`s eye is opened
And I can see everywhere

Music is life
I thought I was dead
until I hear the music
Playing in my head

What are you saying?
I can`t hear you

Never heard a word
You said
This music got me going
Even deeper instead

Leon Pryce

Lullaby

The spirals of her brain
are like a millions trains
travelling on the OCD highway

In the dark
eyes are closed
but the jaw has clenched
and thoughts have not
been quite cleansed
the generator still on overload

She longs for
a carbon monoxide high
at least one tranquil
moment to sleep
when every medicinal treat
does nothing but make
her body weak

Until lo and behold
it was a remedy
right under her nose
a lightly pluck of strings
a gentle tapping
of concerto tones
woodwind melodies
to seep deep in the bones

sounds meant to utilize

when angels fly

the classics
have become her lullaby

Donna J. Sanders

Rhymes Rebirth

They going to hear rhymes they never heard before
It will come as a rap beat, right down to Biggie and Tupac
So slick and hardcore
I am the rebirth
I am like an angel that walks the earth
I revolutionized
I am the element of surprise
Read my script like an animation on paper
For this new millennium
I plan to start the New Year
As a fresh poet and poetical rapper
With a little more style and more grammar
So do not mistake me for those wannabees
I will work my ass off to fulfill my destiny
I will never sell my soul
To achieve the worlds gold and vanity
However, I stay true and conscious
Because I know, I am precious
With Christ, I grow old
I am black and bold

My rhymes are a combination of words and grammar
A few misfits, an editor would penalized
However, when you check my style
A gift you just cannot deny
I do not beg for recognition
I do not kiss asses to gain fame or do self-proclamation
I am the phantom that will earn my respect
In print my name is engraved
My path is paved; many are called
But only a few is chosen by God
Against all the odd
Connect my analogy

I am a poetical Genius
My lyrics are as a composed orchestrated
Musical rhapsody
Call me prodigy
I am the rebirth of Modern Rhymery.

Christena AV Williams

Soundtrack

The music of my youth still sings to me.
Inside my head it still plays Dylan and Baez
as part of our song, our time, our places.
Subversive music, coming from the streets.
Out of tune with the surround sound monotone.
Undermining it with a discordant challenge.

Harmony and discord,
the songs of peace and love
sitting side by side with war and revolution.
Then as now they still speak to us,
still sing in tune
The lyrical passion of the words,
the movement music of the songs,
has crossed our time and space.
Melodies of movement
which still can break our boundaries
and join us back together.
Moving rhythms which still excite
and words which dance for us.

These moving patterns on a page,
have make different music now,
wrapped in our emotions and melodies
which have few boundaries
and are timeless and placeless
when in tune with changing times,
which for us, can be any time at all.

Lynn White

Poetic Melodies

Poetic Melodies

Harmonies

Poetic Melodies

Sunshine Song

Sitting here
I sing for you
a song of
morning sunshine,
chirping from
my little lungs
a yellow flower symphony.

Soon enough
your siren call
will echo
through the airwaves,
dancing with
a compass rose
to guide me home and nest.

Scott Thomas Outlar

When She Sings

When she sings, she channels all that she's heard
Raising to tiptoe and warbling like a morning bird
She sounds as beautiful as the rush of angel wings
This is my little songbird, glorious when she sings

When she sings, there's no telling what you'll hear
Raised around country folks drinking beer
I'll tell you of one who was her crazy old uncle
Who was particularly fond of Simon and Garfunkel
Another, an ex-boyfriend, who loved ol Hank and Cash
And was known to go cheating after smoking hash
She'll easily belt out a drinking and cheating song
Raising the roof with a voice classic and strong
Then drop to a whisper and sing Amazing Grace
That will leave wonderment all over your face
"Go Rest High On That Mountain" or "Whiskey Lullaby"
And I promise the room will have nary a dry eye
Born with a blessed gift, she sings from a pure heart
When she looks at you and sings it will rip you apart

When she sings, she channels all the abuse she's felt
Pours it into every vibrant note her voice can belt
Haunting as the brush of unseen angel wings
This is my little songbird, glorious when she sings

I can never hold her; I'd damage her healing wings
So I listen in rapture to my songbird when she sings
I pay the barkeep for her a round or two
Then I slip out the door when her set is through
Echoes of her melodies haunt me as I walk
Every night with my demons I have a little talk
So far I have won and will as long as I am strong
I won't let my darkness hurt my songbird and her song

Poetic Melodies

For my salvation comes twice a week
When into the Horseshoe I quietly sneak
Listen to her angelic voice make the rafters ring
For my salvation comes when she sings

D. B. Hall

The Poet's Harmony

Let me sing you a song.
Listen in close.
This is the melody
Of a poetic host.
I'm strumming my words
Just like a guitar.
The vibrations form
In syllable bars.
Sing along out loud
Or only in your mind.
The poet's harmony
Is rhythm and rhyme.

Christopher Allen Breidinger

Switchblade Songbird

Switchblade songbird
Sing me a song
Make it quick and sharp
So I can sing along

Sing about love
And then about hate
Sing it now
Don't hesitate

Sing sharp keys
Sing em quick
Make me sing too
That's the trick

Sing low keys
Sing em slow
Sing in a way
That steals the show

Sing a song
That moves my feet
Sing me something
Really sweet

Sing of faith
Sing of God
Sing a song that
Makes my head bob

But when I'm blue
Slow it way down
A nobody move

Poetic Melodies

Stickup sound

Sing something country
With a sadness deep
Maybe a song
About lost sheep

Switchblade songbird
Haven't you heard
Don't sing me any
Disparaging words

Sweet little Switchblade
Songbird by name
You're as quick as a switch
And sharp as a blade

To make you sing slow
Is all my own blame
You were made to sing
Fast and sharp
As per your name

So pick it up why don't cha
And sing how you were made
Don't mind me
And the slow request
I have made.

Billy Charles Root

Molded in Song

I let melodies erode
The contours I've always known
In broad, beaming harmonies
Where I gleefully wither alone

Marred by sound
Wrecked by the swell of verse
I happily decay
Consigned, to the depths of their curse

Let shorelines abate
To be maimed by majestic tone
To be swayed in its bloom
And be courted to a bliss not shown

William L. Wright, Jr.

Music in the House

There are many sounds in the house.
With Love, they become music.

The father has to work from home
and taps on the keyboard.

The mother mixes her dinner
with a spatula and taps it on the sauce pan.

The grandfather entertains
and excites the little one.

The grandmother sings to the kids
and keeps them enthralled.

The maid hums
while dusting and cleaning.

The gardener waters the plants
and sprinkles it around.

The newborn fusses and
the mother rushes to him

The kids play in the backyard
and have fun together.

The birds dance and sing
happily near the feeder

The water falls in the fish tank
and the bubbles float together.

The wind chimes together
dances in the breeze.

The kiddo takes his bath
and splashes around in the tub

Sunayna Pal

Melodious in B Major

After the melodious 'sound of silence'
that which comes nearest to
expressing the inexpressible.
touching the untouchable;
burning it's way into your heart
is simply... Music.

Ken Allan Dronsfield

I dream in Symphonies

Beyond the sunset my
melodious thoughts
and anxieties melt into
an ensemble of symphonic
sequences, canton consequences
neon nuances – At first all sound is
abafando, masterly muted even muffled
whilst distant galactic pulses surge with
a capriccio free to find their own tempo
creating a hollow halo then suddenly as I
float adrift I detect distant bursts of
energy exploding with accentato
emphasizing a solar legacy – I cannot
help but move my shoulders to the intergalactic
beat tingling my feet, as it is so ballabile quite
fantastical even undeniably danceable – now
I'm falling through a strange vortex, swirling
whirling hearing an unidentified bisbigliando, a faint
whispering as I strangely begin to sing in calando
falling away fading – instantaneously I'm blinded
by stellar bodies brillante, sparkling harmoniously
heightening my dormant auditory impulses
as I realize I'm swallowing sound, singing
bocca chiusa with a closed mouth my inner shouts -
Am I still breathing my heart beating in perfect
timing or am I suffering sorrowfully in dark dolente?
Is our rhythm becoming estinto extinguished extinct?
My inner pulse now floating grazioso slowly becoming
mancando but I refuse to die away – This dream concert
was meant for me, meant for nocrurne, meant for the
endless night as it slows down to niente, barely audible
yet still filled with penseroso, thoughtfully blending
new melodies peu à peu, little by little the sounds will cease

Poetic Melodies

in a motoin of scorrevole, gliding from note to note
until it all becomes eerily tacet, silent
as I slip away larghissimo, very slowly leaving this
splendid show feeling quite devoto, religiously
remembering my beginning as I become libero
set free to my last musical reverie, my final ommagio
to celebrate this earthly journey I was put on -
so if I seem pensive even sometimes malinconico
do not let my melancholy mute my inner melody
as I dream in symphonies

Don Beukes

Unsung Sonnet

I heard a spontaneous sonnet
sound itself from my lips

I didn't stop for even one second
to try to write it down.

Instead I just let its acoustics
float off into the air

a present for my solitude and the Universe itself.

Heath Brougher

Secluded Notes

I found seclusion
Between ear budded headphones
They took me to a place of calming drift
Poetry in motion as if a train ride away
Escape momentarily into a small piece
of peace

Eyes close soft and light
While ears absorb the vibes and rhymes
My heart beats within the rhythm
Synchronized with each drum beat
Eye twitches go to steady dark stare

The black and whites come in slow
Cascading tones of fingers trickle over
Ebony and ivory keys of soul elsewhere
And I am caught up into the third heaven
Consciousness of where am I
Is eclipsed by acoustic reverberations

like seasonings on sustenance
A salting of steel chords begins mixing
The multitude of coursing sounds Rescue me
Not out of body but out of world
I am present, but not wholly here

For the duration of the piece
I am taken away from silence and sound
For all there is , is the music
Strums, beats and taps massage my thoughts
And for a moment
I am one with the vibrations

Poetic Melodies

I am the bass drums hollow holler
I am the pickups of electrified six strings
I am the blending of the piano keys
I am become the music
Lost in secluded notes

Billy Charles Root

Rhythm

There still are some things
That are natural
Things which you cannot deny
Still some things
That can't be man-made
Like the sun, the trees and the sky

Through whispering canyons
Along waterfall lines
Searching for the wherefore and the why
If you want
You can close your eyes
But don't let the natural pass you by

And . . .
Rhythm . . . is something that's natural
Rhythm is something that's real
Rhythm is something you're born with
Rhythm is something you feel

You don't know how it comes out of you
You feel it comes from above
I don't know . . . It's something inside of you
Rhythm is something like love

There are natural things
That you can find
No matter where you go
There is all the time
And all the places
To learn what there is to know

But in all these things

Poetic Melodies

And all these places
Where do you find the glow
In your life
There is so much to do
And so many feelings to show

And . . .
Rhythm . . . is something that's natural
Rhythm is something that's real
Rhythm is something you're born with
Rhythm is something you feel

You don't know how it comes out of you
You feel it comes from above
Rhythm is something inside of you
Rhythm is something like love

C. Steven Blue

Every Heart has a Poetic Melody

Every heart has a poetic melody.
Doesn't every voice want some form of parity?
Like that alert; spring black bird, flying back and forth
Perched in bough both low and high in treetops and gorse.

Flying unheard to nurture her, own cherished world
Aren't we full of song, aren't we too keeping them hushed?
Waiting just the right moment; in the morn, abrupt
To sing our; hearts out rhythmically, pure and loud.

Isn't every breast full to bursting out in song?
All night long… all year long… all live lifelong.

Mark Andrew Heathcote

Starting Over

The music swells and

The earth shakes – this is music too
A great rumbling from the underbelly
The cries of fear and the humility
Beyond despair

But how do we start over once
The world shook open and
Swallowed us whole?

Music too –
The ocean's roar the rustling
Of Leaves.
There is so much to the movement
Of trees, to the song of the birds
Landing to feed

The music we make!
Its origins wake to sound divine,
Whispering through the melodies
Of thrushes and the harmonies
Of rain

Swallowing our pain we have
Slung to the world from the most
Tender of voices rounding out,

Through the eaves,
The moon-filled night
With fiery sensation so that
We shudder as memories
Come awake

And heave a sigh
Readying to sing again
Until the only
Note is

One.

Tammy T. Stone

Music

Play me the flute of life's repute,
Of all that's good, of love & compassion,
The music of all that's beyond refute,
Of loves platonic & those of passion.

Play me the sitar of gentle chantings,
Of all that's faith & all that's God,
Of the gentle earth & all our plantings,
Of life in water, sky & humble sod.

Play me the drums of ancestors old,
Of all who have passed & those to come,
Resounding messages of nations bold,
Echoing past the moon into the arms of the sun.

Play me the lute, guitar, mandolin, penny-whistle,
Pluck me, strum me & beat me the tune,

Serenade the rose, the oak, the wind-blown thistle,
So all may dance beneath the crystal moon.

But of all the symphonies I wish to hear,
Is that of your voice, now long gone,
Listening with my heart & not my ear,
Lingering in my soul, your eternal song.

Sue Lobo

Among the Unfulfilled

You lead
And I follow devoutly
In pursuit of inner rapture
Bestowed, in each scrap of melody

Enthralled
Lockstep
Ever-loyal

The harmonies pour
In unwavering torrents
A bounty
For scouring hearts
Sprung open, by their savage thirst

Enthralled
Lockstep
Ever-loyal

They'll nurse their young
And vibrant tales
Laboring for the swell
Of crisp, synchronized emotion

You lead
I follow
Ever-true
Among the droves
Dream-brimmed, yet unfulfilled

To reap
And to sow
Our timeless and unified song

Our desperation
Our cold and unheeded refrain

William L. Wright, Jr.

Harmony

We began so well, so in tune,
catching the notes dropped by angels
and playing with them before they fell,
creating a perfect harmony.

But then, we started to miss a few notes
which fell, crashing into our rhythms,
disrupting the flow of our music,
upsetting our harmony.

Just a few at first,
but they violated our space,
causing us to miss our step and
almost fall ourselves.

Then, bar after bar came tumbling down.
Cascades of discords raining down between us.
No longer dropped by angels.
Surely not?

Now we are finished and falling tunelessly.
Lost.
Loudly separated by discords.
Floundering in the storm.
Our past melodies out of reach,
devoid of harmony.

Lynn White

Instruments

Violin

Entranced by the movements
of your flexible bow

filling me with temptations
as your uncurled hair sings

I salivate after the curves
of your varnished ribs

longing to caress the neck
upon which scrolls soar

Oh dear violin

how you seduce my heart
with your constricted strings

melodies too savory
for my soul

Donna J. Sanders

Ode to the Talking Drum

Fair instrument of melody,
I salute the mind you possess,
keeping dance in your custody,
and your own notions you express
separately, among peers in Ayangalu's hands.

Mighty are the rhythms you've got,
conveyed beyond a thousand mile;
you are cousin to the parrot,
and much more for your brilliant style:
revealed in what your cord and your string can do.

Herald angel of Music's Muse,
also mouthpiece for all events;
few are the genres you can't use,
since you've mimed Rock Music's comments:
now I know why all cultures and music are one.

The one drum that can stand alone,
two drumheads that have never failed,
squeezed in my arms changes your tone,
awesome message relayed when played:
while each part tapped produces a different sound.

Interlocking rhythms revealed
through fingers, palms, or curved drum stick;
the cause to rejoice isn't concealed
for Mbalax, to whom you're its wick:
harbinger of telegraph, phone and internet.

Olawale Famodun

Melodic Memories

Steel twang,
As the bar slide glided,
Up and down the strings,
Plucking the right notes,
Making it sing,
That ol' dobro,
Laying on your lap,
A shiny red and silver finish,
Oh how I miss the echo of its melody,
Wafting through the house,
Each chord in conversation with the next,
In the hands of the perfect musician,
My dad could really make it talk.

Elizabeth Daniel

Life Is A Piano

Tune in to the rhythm of the times
the tides dancing and chirping birds sublime
Life's piano keys are overused
and yet can create tones out of the forgotten notes.

The sounds left me breathless
sinking in this world of endless madness
The high pitch often startles me out of the blue
while the low tone leaves a footprint of a different hue.

I look up to the heaven's above
while the music of my heart
is carried by the blowing wind
an overwhelming, calming presence on me reigned.

The piano music filled the tranquil air anew
my thoughts goes out to you casts in a lighted avenue
her angelic voice still lingers in my peaceful serenity
singing in tune with each tempo and melody.

Elizabeth Esguerra Castillo

Finger Jams

I am the cord
that you strum
The vibration of sound
created by your finger tip

The callus,
holds the memory of every note
Sweeping delightfully
along my cord

Together we make music beautifully

Raja Williams

Enchanted Flute

Enchanted flute
you weave a tale
in magical notes
so hearts can sail.
Every listening ear
discerns its song
a beauty complete
when dreams, to hearts belong.
Hesitate not, Enchanted Flute
for dreamers await
to hear from you
their song of fate.

Baidha Fercoq

Poetic Melodies

Fingering Strings

"If a man is considered guilty 4 what goes on in his mind, then give me the electric chair 4 all my future crimes- OH!"—Prince from, Electric Chair, released on the Batman Soundtrack, 1989

Beautiful
amen,

over and
over
again—

lightning
burns
my soul.

Victor Clevenger

Piano

Even when your strings
Are slightly out of tune
The right fingers
On your ivory's
Will transfix
An audience
Even when your gloss
Becomes dull with years
The air will carry
Your beautiful melody
To my waiting ears

Maggie Mae Carter

My Spanish Guitar

I remember being just a child,
Reaching deep into the wild.
Holding a tennis racket in my hand,
Strumming it for my band.
How amused I was as I sang out loud,
In front of an imaginary crowd.
I was the best guitar player in the world,
I was daddy's little girl.
I saw fame like a celebrity,
In the kitchen it was really me.
In my fingers I gripped my guitar pick,
My pretend music notes I picked up quick.
I was the queen in the roaring crowd,
A one girl band singing out loud.
That racket played like a Spanish guitar,
You could hear every string from afar.
How beautiful the sound I sang in tune,
Underneath the neon moon.
Tambourines and flutes in collaboration,
No noise and no distraction.
I was the princess entertaining everyone,
The sweetest instrument under the sun.
Lost on a faraway stage in a field,
This seemed all too real.
My daddy smiled so proudly at me,
I was the triumphant sound in the victory.
The music flowed freely through my veins,
Until I became me again.
The tennis racket was my favorite instrument,
Playing it to my heart's content.
Then one day my daddy went to Spain,
And bought me the real thing.
I desired to touch every chord,

Poetic Melodies

Music sheets covered the floor.
Every note at the tip of my fingers,
The beauty in the sound lingered.
Like a pianist on his throne,
I reigned supreme all alone.
Every part of me strummed to a different beat,
As the world watched the passion in me.
Daddy's little girl played hard every day,
To be the musician he made.
My tennis racket was gone and now far,
Because now I enjoy my Spanish guitar.

Shirley Ann Cooper

First Love

My lover grew up with a guitar in his hands,
playing for his supper with assorted bands.
He can barely remember a time without
the urge to move his long fingers about.
Those strings created melodies so sweet,
his foot tapping each precious beat.
Instruments of wood and nylon thread
would rest in the corner by our double bed.
And, whenever I decided to go far away,
if they couldn't come, then he would stay.
There was a kind of struggle that persisted,
for two attachments of the heart existed.
Yet, I always sensed that if put to a test,
his love for music would override the rest.
So, I embraced the first love of his life,
and settled for being his wife.

Teresa Roberts

Sounds of the Drums

The echoes of the drums
Traveled across the distance
Carrying the messages of those left behind
Transcending the horizons
Of the Atlantic oceans

I hear the drums
I hear the voices of the ancestors
The cries of those on the slave ships
Traveling to the new world

The white man feared
His heart trembled with despair
The boat is unstable on the troubled waters
Of the Caribbean Sea
Because the sound of the drums
Is manipulating the course of time

I hear the sounds of the drum
I hear Africa calling
Africa is calling
I hear freedom singing
each time there`s a pounding
They dance away and rejoice

I'm an African, I'm a free Negro
In a captured land
I'm free to dance, to live
Each time the drums play
I relive the lives of those who died for me

I hear the sounds of the drum
I hear the voice of my people

I hear the rhythms of the Congo
From the distant past of pain and lost
To the future of victory for the black African

Leon Pryce

Spectral Violin

From where does the melody
of a violin's message begin?
Does its origin arise
between harmony of heart and wood
adding depth and richness
to release a timeless song?
How does the violin's bow
know of the exact moment
to shift its loudness
in a whisper to its fragile strings?
Is the magic released
when tension is toned
and dynamic accents lends its hand
to create a spectacular pitch?
Perhaps the magic from a violin's song
is ultimately captured in resolution
when notes of dissonance echo so sharply, our very life's struggle
as we seek and search to find restful balance
and the violin's bow, offers its salubrious consonance.

Baidha Fercoq

Trumpet

when the lone trumpet
plays the first soulful note
all sound and movements
become quiet and still
the beautiful tune
filled with such sorrow
for the loss it denotes
a hero has fallen
may he find peace
in his eternal rest
the trumpet plays on
though your lyrics are forgotten
the hero will remain
in our hearts and minds
every time we hear
you played

Maggie Mae Carter

African Drums

Across green hippoed river bed I heed your call,
Thumping through my brain's foggy ageing wall,
Over the distance of childhood memories, turned to dust,
Reflected within archaic tears of the elephants musth,
Thudding dully on my dark, scratched, echoed soul,
Left long behind, a booming vacant endless hole,
Behind tented sleeping lids, I feel the blistered beat,
The ancient music in my head, stirring my heart, urging my feet,
To sway to the chattering of slapped skin on hand,
To the whispering tongue of the throbbing land,
I feel the caressing kiss of zephyr's dusty breath,
While dancing in my head to ecstasy's sweet death,
It was there I left the child behind; where the bush voice strums,
But the scars remaining deep, are of long-gone African drums.

Sue Lobo

Instrument

An instrument
Is only as good
As its musician
A heart
Is only as good
As its handler
A painting
Is only as good
As its artist
A soul
Is only as good
As its keeper

The violin
Sings its beautiful
Sad song
The heart
Weeps for
The writer
The paint
Never meets
The canvas
The soul
Shutters
At the loss

Maggie Mae Carter

Soul Sounds

Poetic Melodies

Humanity Sings

Humanity sings,
can you hear it ?
In laughter and sighs,
in cries of passion,
in moans of pain.
Humanity sings,
in silent screams,
in the pulse
of a beating heart,
in swaying hips
to a soundless song,
in the rhythmic march
 of soldiers boots,
in a whispered sigh
over a dying dream,
in a gunshot in the dark.
Humanity sings,
of life and death
and everything in between.
of hope and despair,
of love lost
and faith reborn,
of sins redeemed
and passion scorned.
Humanity sings,
in the first clear cry from
a newborn's mouth,
in a cry of triumph
or a whimper of defeat,
in a desperate plea to heaven,
in the quiet acceptance of death,
in a jubilant song of praise,

Poetic Melodies

or the silent solitude of prayer.
Can you hear,
Humanity sing?

Tamsen Grace

Music at Dusk

Dusk is so sexy
with no set time of day
It's when people come out
to party and play
as the guitar man starts to strum
people sway to the beat of the drums
and let the sweet peal of the sax
move them on into the night
under the bright neon light.

I love this seductive time
but under a different dusk
with different music
that I feel in my bones
with a slow rising moon
I listen to tree frogs croon
crickets chirp
an old coyote howls
he's hungry and on the prowl
even sometimes an occasional owl
it's sweet music to my ears.

Then dark comes on full bore
and silence
becomes so still
throw a couple of logs on the fire
let those flames flare up
turn on some late night tunes
pull my baby in tight
dance ever so close
and slow

let those flames flare up
my baby nibbles as she whispers
"Honey, I love you"
it's soul music to my ears.

D. B. Hall

Nature's Opus

The storm is an echo of
what ravaged space and time
eating away at bliss sublime
 a deep growl signals it
it knows it – The rumblings
like percussion drums
apologizing mesmerizing
rising above
scaring a lonely dove.

The rising waves a challenge
like bass over baritone
soprano over alto then
another sudden salvo as
a watery beast is let loose
causing murky mayhem
exacting its own wild wrath
evolving expanding evaporating.

The fire a mezzo soprano delivering
a fierce performance rising in destructive
tone cutting to the bone causing a hopeless
frown as amber flecks spit and scowl
in perfect staccato leaving no doubt of
their end goal turning green to charcoal.

The wind an ensemble of different tunes
a weeping cello lamenting its isolation
a weary oboe announcing misery and mystery
whilst a recorder innocently supports the whole
a new goal, still on the sidelines no real guides.

Auditory wailing hides the off key events

the unseen subsidence the silent killer
our demise our own doing causing man-made
flooding – life's rapids a brief warning knell
of the carnage to come, whilst future calm clouds
prevent devastating rip roaring epic events.

Nurture it
appreciate it
understand it
live with it
protect it
sing with it
feel with it...

Don Beukes

The Voice of Heart

Music –the voice of heart
full of rhythm and melody.
Music expresses various moods.
Love (shringar), Comic (hasya),
Heroic (veera), terrible (bhayanak),
Sadness (Karuna), furious (rudra),
Disgust (vibhats), wonder (adbhuta) and Peace (shanta).
Music expresses the love of life.
A feeling of solace,
Music acts as remedy to pain and suffering.
Music is a connecting link
that combines the entire world together.

Rashmi Jain

Celestial Crescendo

Opera of God –
dancing rhythmic stars alight
singing sirens sigh

Scott Thomas Outlar

Background Noise

Melodious memories creep up and down, in and around,
mountain high, valley low, a prelude to the deafening colors
vibrantly bursting open my chest.

Universal language beyond words, you speak without verse,
bereft of race and nationality, an identity that resides
within the secret fathoms of me.

Singing souls brought together to be torn asunder,
the maleficent ocean to the tranquil shore, wavelengths to endure
and explore my unchartered depths.

Inspiration erases doubts and fears of lost innocence,
free of inhibitions the spirits dance, maddeningly, a moth to a quivering flame,
slowly but surely driving me insane.

Creating harmonies that soar with powerful crescendos,
afloat with healing words and hurtling towards an everlasting hope,
that we may cross the boundaries we call home.

L. J. Diaz

Music of Life

Music existed along with the creation of earth
The primitive sound 'Om' gave rise to various notes.
Music is the food of life,
Present in every slice of life.
From the twittering of birds to the rustling of leaves,
The sound of cataract to the humming of bees,
The drops of rain or symphony of orchestra,
From the lullaby of mother to the recitation of
ritualistic mantra,
Music is enwrapped in everything.
Music -the happiness of heart and soul,
symbolizing purity despite all the odds.
Music is a bridge, a connecting note not only to gods
but paves path of peace and harmony for all.

Rashmi Jain

Dancing to a Heart Song

She carries her umbrella,
but only for a bright Sun;
Loving the falling rain as
it gently kisses her face.
Dancing to a heart song;
a sweet embracing hug.
My little bit of heaven,
courting a stylish waltz.
Tune my soul with sonnets
of rhyming loved melodies.
A pious and angelic touch,
with me now, upon a breeze.

Ken Allan Dronsfield

Musical String Theory

Created to be a living entity, the cosmos erupted as a single sound. To see expansion fueling growth is really quite profound. Newly forming hydrogen produces a string with its own tone. Ancient dust from gigantic distant stars now resides within our bones.

The human race are far too young, to do much more than to observe. Like an infant in its cradle, crying for attention it feels it should deserve. And like that infant so young and new, we are the center of all we know. One day we'll gain maturity, exit from our crib, and begin to see the show.

We each are one tiny string, coiled up within itself, disconnected, on a ridge. We must uncoil and connect with all the other strings to form a lasting bridge. Like synapses in our brains connect one inkling to another, to form a thought. If we cannot abide in this connectedness, our struggles are all for naught.

When connected, the strings resonate in harmony, beginning a new song.

Valormore De Plume

Music of the Monsoons

The raindrops sound their strings
Over antique rooftops,
Supplying solace and symphony
To the parched terrains.

The thunders bellow in high notes
And it seems like the last yells
Of a dying Indian summer.

Retreating birds in clusters fly
And sing mellifluous tunes of glee,
Adding more sweetness
To the honeyed song of Nature.

And at night, the passionate frogs
Croon lovely lays in a chorus,
Lulling the hamlet towards slumber.

The ebb and flow of the babbling brooks
Hum sweet lyrics in rapturous ripples,
While the trees and the breeze
Perform amorous acrobatics,
Reveling in a display of song and dance.

The raindrops, the thunders, the birds,
The frogs, the brooks and the breeze
Are in fact Nature's indelible instruments,
That impeccably produce
The music of the monsoons.

Debasish Mishra

Spirituality

The best of everything
Is offered to God

Be it art,
Architecture
Or, Music

Music is the lubricant
Of every religion
It is woven into
Rites and rituals

Devotional songs
Had a niche market
On gramophone records
Tapes, CDs, DVDs
And, now, on internet

Hymns for Christians
Kawalis for Muslims
Bhajans for Hindus
Chants for Buddhists
Kirtans for Sikhs
So on and so forth

Whether it is the Church
Or Masjid
Or Mandir
Or Monastry
Or Gurudwara
Or, any other place of worship,
Most rituals ride on music

There is some supernatural power
That drives the whole universe
Our best offerings are devoted
And dedicated to that power
When music reaches that power
And, touches the heart and soul
Of that Supreme Being
Music achieves spirituality

Vincent Van Ross

The Calling

If you, too, have felt the pulsating beat
in your solar plexus, behind your temples
If you feel the need to withdraw, retreat,
wander the forests or city streets.
If the music of a night full of moonlight
pulls at your heart strings,
then you may be a witch.
Don't fight it
Take delight in it.

If you, too, can wail at the moon
Beat the drums and play the pipes
If you sing a song that woos the loon
Makes the men around you fall and swoon
If darkness covers your face without a trace
of spine-tingling fear,
then you may be a witch
Don't fight it
Delight in it

Yes, it's a calling, a witch is chosen
And, the music created is saturated
with magic, wild and sweet
So, just let go, my wonderful, witchy friend
Follow the notes to the amazing end
And, please….
Don't fight it
Delight in it!

Teresa Roberts

Soul Strumming

Vibrations in the
pool of existence

Yearn to achieve higher
resonance within the universal
play that is called existence

Music moves through us
because we are living, breathing
metronomes

A change in tempo quickly
reflects our heartbeat as
we move to the next
concerto

Let us recognize
that nothing that is

should be different

And that the rhythm
of being will always be
present in the cosmic
beat that is life

Adam Levon Brown

Poetic Melodies

Artist Tributes

Song for Karen

The inner voice of a multitude
your words and aching lamentation
comforted generations still to soothe
melting hearts liquefying emotions

You once bid farewell to love
claimed no-one ever cared
if you should live or die
would we now hear one more cry?

A fixed smile barred your pain
what if you only once shared the strain?
You sang of sweetest dreams come true
glaring into eyes that adored you
asking let me be the one
yearning for a loving touch
how you longed to see the sun
the emptiness and lonely void too much

Oh how your universe sparkled
you felt on top of the world
he made your feelings fly
and shone his starlight down on you

As each last note was played
you realized every promise he made
broke before long at the end of each song
how you searched for a place
to hide away

Your loneliness oh what a sad affair
if only he promised a lifetime to share
a heart punctured your essence fading

finding the right one
an eternal craving

There was nothing so hard
as convincing your brittle heart
that time would ease the pain
your dwindling health such a shame

Your loved ones dear
misunderstood your fear
they pleaded you leave
your sadness behind
how you sometimes longed to quit
yet your blessed voice
would not admit

You were love's greatest non-believer
yet you saw the wonder
in most everything
you left a beautiful
lasting legacy

The radio still
preaching your fantasy…

Don Beukes

One World In Harmony

YOU try so hard to make them understand

MAY the peace we seek be at our command

SAY what you will, they just won't make a stand

THAT is the dilemma always in my hand

I'M a dreamer of peace, I've always been

A knower that with war we will never win

DREAMER of a kind that grew up knowing

BUT surrounded by people who just stopped growing

I'M not trying to criticize, I'm just trying to say

NOT another single war can ever save the day

THE violence just brings more, it's the nature of the biz

ONLY peace can bring peace, that's just the way it is

ONE WORLD IN HARMONY, SHARING AND CARING WITH COMPASSION FOR ALL

C. Steven Blue

Quotation Acrostic ~ My quote is by John Lennon: "You may say that I'm a dreamer, but I'm not the only one."

Purple

his songs sink
deep into my soul
the music and lyrics
move my body and mind
his melodies
sooth the chaos
of my days and nights
bringing euphoric feelings to light
the Prince
with the purple heart
filled to overflowing with love
a talent that may never be out shined
the Heavens
wept with us mortals
as you flew away to new heights
may the angels rejoice at your sight

Maggie Mae Carter

My Quest

I never met Bonita Applebaum
but I've been serenaded with the song
it didn't turn me on but we danced all night long
I'd visit El Segundo if I had a chance
wouldn't leave my wallet but I would
drop a phone number and hope he'd call it
wondering can we kick it hoping he'd say yes we can
I was taller than a 5 footer and he was a six-foot man
we both loved real hip hop when it was flawless
now they marketing garbage hip hop or whatever they call it
so we created a scenario of electric relaxation
and every song he played was a dedication
I bust a few rhymes to go with it
he said Oh my God I didn't know you were a poet
let me lay a beat for you to flow with
yeah we got the jazz mixed with a little pizzazz
yall on point is what people said as they went pass
I'm on point all the time in my mind
as he was on point with the rhythmic bass lines
in the end we extracted the abstract
with the memory of Bonita Applebaum on the playback.

Salute to A Tribe Called Quest

Veronica "Vee" Thornton

Eazy-E

Eazy-E
A strong voice of his time
But it wasn't just his motivating rhymes
It was the fight against cops and their crimes
He helped with the case of Rodney King
But of course the judge just gave it a swing
So the case was lost
But Eazy didn't get so soft
His lyrics about blacks being discriminated continue
But a beat and rhythm wouldn't solve the issue
It wasn't until after the death if Eazy-E people started to change
It took the death of a man to see it was time for a new age
So look into his lyrics and then you'll see
God bless the memory of Eazy-E

Isiah Williams

Ode to Jimi Hendrix

I love the spirit of Jimi
And the essence of his soul.
Felt forever in the notes he played
And his words, like liquid gold.
A treasure always worth seeking,
In the breaking of a mold,
As the love of power goes to past
And the power of love takes hold.

Christopher Allen Breidinger

The Man

The rhythm to the method you can't mess with
He left tracks on my brain
like I came to Bring the Pain
I knew why he was All I Needed to Get By
And I never asked How High
If I heard Redman was stopping by
together we could touch the sky
I know some don't understand
Why I love The M-E-T-H-O-D Man
He was just always my favorite from
The Wu-Tang Clan
a handsome, articulate multi-talented man
never to be a crazy fan
I just admire, appreciate and love the methods of
The M-E-T-H-O-D Man.

Veronica "Vee" Thornton

Love Letter to the Beatles

In My life, I've had a love affair with the Beatles.

Here, There And Everywhere, they've enchanted and moved the world with their music.

They started a *Revolution*.

I couldn't wait to jump aboard the magical mystical tour

with stop offs at *Penny Lane* and *Strawberry Fields*.

My dream like journey continued along The Long And Winding Road

and ended at an octopus's garden in the shade.

With Lonesome Tears In My Eyes, I now sit by my turntable surrounded by old friends

dressed in shiny black vinyl.

In attendance are lovely Rita, *Eleanor Rigby* and *Sergeant Pepper*, amongst others.

Hey Jude starts to play and it's like the stylus has pierced my vein, flowing the purest

of lyrics and melody into my once empty soul.

I wake up feeling *Free As A Bird*,

With A Little Help From My Friends.

My heart gently weeped the day John and George said goodbye forever.

I cried out let it not be!

Imagine they're in heaven.

It's easy if you try.

Leading an angels choir,

what a joyous sound that must be.

Kelly Klein

Comfortably Numb

As I sit on a moving train feeling comfortably numb,
My hands can't help but feel the pounding drums.
I'm so lost in the studio sound,
The high above the ground.
The wall comes tumbling down like Pink Floyd,
A struggle I cannot avoid.
I try to place another brick in the wall,
Only to find yet another fall.
So where do I run from this crazy life,
The chaos behind these cold eyes.
A vivid legacy ready to come to,
A bizarre Pink to Blue.
In this disaster of a world,
How can one save a troubled girl.
While she awaits to be number one,
She sits on a moving train feeling comfortably numb.

Shirley Ann Cooper

Cry Goodbye

Ruby-lipped legend,
Miss honky-tonk divine~
Let's sing again of
Lonesome heartache,
Plead it clearly,
Patsy Cline.

With time,
The pain in
Lessons lessen,
Dare we recall
The sad, blue sights?

When we'd walk,
Damsel-desperate…
Beneath the moon,
After midnight?

Oh, Darlin',
If you're crazy~
Then surely so am I…

We weren't first to fall
For fools-gold love,
And aren't the last left to
Cry blessed goodbyes.

Christa Frazee

Ode To Mridangam Master

Oh hail! Musical warrior of the gods
Resounding divine rhythms
Across the heavens,
As you strike the periphery in style
Yaksha and Yakshini
Deliver oceans of trinity,
Your hands and feet are in symphony
 Your power as a King
Through the timbres of clay, limbs and goatskin,
Spawning aesthetically.
You regenerate paralleling patterns
Of mathematics of the deities,
You are the ensemble
Of the musical heritage
The protector of percussion's epic.

Caroline Nazareno-Gabis (Ceri Naz)

Mars Piper: A Poem For Syd Barrett

A piper from Mars
You created amorphous soundscapes
While revolving lights projected
Onto the myriad patterns
Of your tie-dye shirts

You chanted out rhymes
Drawn from nursery playrooms
To make fairy tales in song form

Then your mind overloaded
As you took too many sugar lumps
In order to escape from the fallout shelter of reality
So you could experience the inner workings of
An orange, a plum and a matchbox.

Your guitar feedback squalls
Became screams of war
Detuning on stage
To leave Arnold, Emily and Matilda
Back in the darkroom of your mind

Then the band went on without you
So you made solo acts to express
Your divergent landscapes
Becoming a music press legend

Soon you went back home

Poetic Melodies

To focus on non-musical canvases
Once made – then destroyed

Still you will forever be
A true pioneer
of Psychedelic Art-Rock.

Julius Howard

Poetic Melodies

Under the Influence of Bob Marley

I am under the influence, herbal meditation
Come and jam with us
Cause we jamming
Feeling irie
I am under the influence
Some soul searching
Knowledge impartation
Some spiritual purification
Radical meditation
There is a natural mystic blowing through the air
If you listen carefully then you will hear
Like a drummer I am rocking to the beat
A beat of a reggae legend
Talking blues, so sweet
Under the influence I feel like smoking some herbs
I feel like bombing
Do not mistake me for a terrorist
Because I is of righteousness
However, I will not stand while prophets are killed
While I keep silent and watch
It is brighter on the outside than really it is
On the inside
I emulate the freedom fighters
I am here to elevate and break down barriers
I am here to speak my mind without fear
I am under the influence of Bob Marley.

Christena AV Williams

Gardenia

Lady sings straight passion blues...
The kind that soothes Tragedy's bruises~
Melodically-rare, mending-repair,
Of what some inherit, already broken.

Weeping willow for the sorrow, Child~
Tender sass to pass the storms awhile…
Sipping nectars of man-made poison;
To numb the sting of stolen dreams within.

Some never know those levels of raw hell...
Never seeing beyond learned masks or veil...
This woman was phenomenal, romantic rebellion~
This woman battled demons, in rags or finest satin.

Billie brought it in brawl with her own moaning angels~
On stage or in love despite abuse and cruel scandals...
Blossom-crowned, jazzed and jeweled, in infamous style,
Lady sang straight passion blues, rare rhythm undeniable.

Christa Frazee

Tracy Chapman

This inspirational black folk singer
With a deep spiritual message,
Love and passion for humanity
As driven me to explore the human existence.
Her unique and poetic style
As inspired me to go
Deeper in me to find those
Secret message I behold
Which I wish to share with the world

Tracy Chapman is truly great within
Her own way
Her beautiful smile
And charisma is astounding
And that melodious voice
Can full a stadium
The way she plays the guitar
And sings out her heart
I must say she speaks to the
Soul

Tracy Chapman is one of the greatest singers
However, unfortunately she is underrated
I want to let her know
That her work on earth
Was not in vain
As many are with her and because of her music
I began to live for a purpose
Do not give up the fight
Your music cannot die
It lives on in the hearts of man

I see God's beauty in your music
And His reflection in your face

Christena AV Williams

I'm In Love With A Country Man: Homage to John Denver

I´m in love with a country man,
With Smokey Mountains in his eyes,
And sunshine within his golden hair,
With his gaze upon the distant skies.

I´m in love with a country man,
With old Kansas forever on his mind,
And bluegrass deep within his heart,
He´s from where folk are good & kind.

I´m in love with a country man,
Who´s soul´s embedded in God´s good earth,
Who´s music is harmonica, guitar & old banjo,
Who promised to die in the land of his birth.

I´m in love with a country man,

Like all who were serenaded by his song,
And now he lives in Heaven's ranch of God,
But through his music, he´s never really gone.

Sue Lobo

Poetic Melodies

Janis

Every time
we listen,
a little piece
of her heart
cries out.

Lynn White

Poetic Melodies

Epilogue

Publishing Assistance

Starving Artist

In 2013 Ms. Raja Williams realized that there was a gap, a void if you will, within the publishing industry. A writer either had to come up with hundreds, sometimes thousands of dollars to release a book or take on the journey of self-publishing alone. There was no middle ground, no one there to assist, either financially or lead the way in self-publishing. Most writers do not have the finances to pay a publisher, and some don't know where to start when it comes to self-publishing, nor are they prepared to be in business for themselves.

Raja was inspired to start a fund to assist writers in becoming published authors at either a discounted rate or a full publishing scholarship. To begin this fund Raja paid for the publishing of our first anthology Love, a Four Letter Word. Comprised of poets from all around the world. The sales generated from the purchases of the book were placed into a fund that enabled us to fund future publishing's.

Poetic Melodies

We now are able to offer anthology publications, a chance for authors to have a voice in the literary world yearly, and we have been able to offer several authors full scholarships, as well as offering deep discounted publishing services as a whole. We are thankful for the continued support of this program by both our readers and writers alike.

For More Information Please Visit Our Website At:

www.ctupublishinggroup.com/starving-artist-fund.html

Creative Talents Unleashed

Get Connected With Us!

Website: Creative Talents Unleashed Publishing Group

www.ctupublishinggroup.com

Facebook: Get connected with us on our Facebook Page

www.Facebook.com/Creativetalentsunleashed

Twitter: https://twitter.com/CTUPublishing

Blog: www.creativetalentunleashed.com

Pinterest: https://www.pinterest.com/creativetalents/

Instagram: https://instagram.com/ctupublishinggroup/

Tumblr: http://creativetalentsunleashed.tumblr.com/

Creative Talents Unleashed

Creative Talents Unleashed is an independent publishing group that offers writers an opportunity to share their writing talents with the world. We are committed to fostering and honoring the work of writers of all cultures. Our publishing group offers writing tips to assist writers in continued growth and learning, daily writing prompts and challenges to keep the writers mind sharp and challenged, marketing and events, as well as a variety of yearly publishing opportunities. We are honored to be assisting writers in the journey of becoming published authors.

www.ctupublishinggroup.com

For More Information Contact:

Creativetalentsunleashed@aol.com

www.ingramcontent.com/pod-product-compliance
Lightning Source LLC
Chambersburg PA
CBHW071516040426
42444CB00008B/1671